My Life
as an
Over-comer

ROSE GORDON

ISBN 9798730746770 (Paperback)

Printed in the United States of America

happyselfpublisher.com

Contents

Introduction

Life at times can be challenging, yet it can also be so wonderful and full of excitement and joy when you have chosen the way of Jesus! What I'm going to share with you is going to blow your mind. My life as an overcomer has brought me to a place in life where all I can do is rejoice, because God has been so good to me and has brought me through so many circumstances that involved loneliness, sickness, and also spiritual warfare. The word of God says in Ephesians 6:12 that we wrestle not against flesh and blood, but against principalities, against powers, against the rulers of darkness of this world, against spiritual wickedness in high places.

But in 2 Chronicles 20:15, the Lord says, "Be not afraid nor dismayed by reason of this great multitude; for the battle is not yours but God's." In everything I did, I had to depend solely upon God. Before making the next move in my life I had to seek God's guidance. Also for a season, I experienced heavenly things from the spirit of God. I know that I wouldn't be alive if it wasn't for my Lord sustaining me. It is such a blessing that I am alive to share this miraculous personal experience with my readers. Some of these experiences that I have faced and overcame will help you to have a better perspective about life and will also motivate you to be strong and follow your dreams and to also bring to your awareness that God is real and the devil is real too.

This definitely is not something to be taken lightly. People need to follow their dreams and walk in their God-given calling just like I did regardless of what others may say because people will sometimes discourage you or try to lead you into a different direction from the calling of God. I'm now a Pastor, prophetess, and a life coach. God uses me to reach out to people about the gospel and he also uses me in the prophetic anointing. I enjoy serving God and serving others. I also enjoy coaching people, because I believe there are many hurting people out there who need encouragement and empowerment so whatever you do, make sure you follow the leading of God just like I did and let God's will be done in your life.

CHAPTER 1

My Childhood

My life was not a bed of roses. I didn't have the fancy car, or the luxurious house, or the sweet loving husband, or a bank account full of money. But a few things that I did have in my life that I would never trade or replace for anything or anyone in the world is Jesus and my three beautiful daughters. Both Jesus and my children mean the whole world to me. When I was left alone, the Lord was with me in the midst of my loneliness. When I was feeling discouraged, the Lord was there to give me his joy and my children were also there to give me a hug and say "Mom, we love you!"

Now I'm going to begin to tell you a little about myself and my childhood before I accepted Jesus Christ as my Lord and Savior. I was born in Kingston, Jamaica, I am the sixth child out of eight children. I am the youngest of four sisters and I have four brothers. Most of my family lived in St. Mary, which is the country side of Jamaica, and that's where I would go during my break from school and I'm telling you when I'm there that's when the adventure really begins. My family and I would go to the river and wash our clothes, and we would also go fishing and we would catch river shrimps.

After that, we would go for a swim in the river. When nighttime would come, my family and I would take the river shrimp and make soup with it and begin our entertainment for the night. Some nights the full moon is out and the stars are glistening brightly in the clear night skies. Often times we would play fun games such as cricket. We would also stay up and tell funny stories and we wouldn't go to bed until the next morning.

My grandfather was a pastor for a small church and he is very strict when it comes to the things of God. Most of the children that attended my grandfather's church didn't wear any shoes on their feet because their parents were very poor that they could not afford to buy shoes for their children. So it became the norm for some of these children to come to church with bare feet. At one point, I was trying to follow the children by not wearing any shoes on my feet simply because they were also my friends and I didn't want to be the only one who had shoes on. Some of the parents could not even afford new clothes for their children but I remained friends with them.

In church, I didn't always understand what my grandfather preached but I still listened. After church was finish, my friends and I would play outside the church and then afterward we would go home and by the time we reach home our meal was already prepared. Normally, before we begin eating our meal, my cousins and I have to make sure we have clean water to drink and to wash the dishes. If water were not there, we would have to get buckets and bottles to catch the water at the spring.

It surely was a joy for us when it would rain because we didn't have to worry about filling up the large buckets with water! At some point, it was fun to go out and get the water from the spring with my cousins because we would turn it into a fun activity rather than a chore by splashing the water on one another. The only part that I didn't like that much was when we had to climb up the hills with the water buckets on our head.

Certain times of the year, I would go to Ocho Rios to visit my uncle. Uncle Joe was a fisherman. He sold some of the best fish from snapper to salmon, to king fish. He sold just about any type of fish, name the fish, and he had it. Fresh from the sea! Ocho Rios is a tourist resort; it has beautiful scenery, full of life and color from the trees to the very fruits on the tree. My uncle's wife and I would go down to the tourist resort to sell straw hats and straw baskets for the tourists. My uncle's wife owned a small business. I helped sew the patterns to the baskets and the hats, and that helped me to exercise my creative side.

After a long workday with my aunt at her business, my cousins and I would go to the beach to take a swim, kick back, and enjoy ourselves. After our swim, we would go down to the Duns River Fall, which is a river that flows right into the sea and that's where my cousin and I usually go to wash the salt water off our bodies after a swim at the beach.

CHAPTER 2

Returning to Kingston

After returning to Kingston, things just didn't feel the same. I was already missing St. Mary. It came to a point that I was literally begging my parents to let me live there. "Mom and Dad, please, please, please let me stay in the country," I would say to them. But did they listen? No, not really, at least not yet. Their first response was "Rosie, I know that you enjoy your visits in the country, but this is where you live and we don't want you out of our sights for too long." But I couldn't accept that answer. So I continued to beg and persuade until I receive the answer I was looking for. I just didn't want to live in Kingston anymore. I was tired of the same boring day-to-day lifestyle.

What I loved about being in the country compared to living in Kingston is that I always had something to do, there was more entertainment, and most of the people were very friendly, so it wasn't too hard to make friends. After a while, my parents finally agreed to let me go back to St. Mary. They enrolled me into a Catholic school in the countryside and eventually I began to go to the Catholic church.

What do you know I was back to doing my usual routine when I come to visit during the holidays, but the only difference is that it was now permanent and this time I wasn't enjoying myself. I am now officially a resident and not a visitor. I was really looking forward to this special moment. I begged my parents to let me come back to the country and now I'm back and it's just not the same anymore, I was bored out of my mind. So one day I decided to write a letter and send it to my parents in Kingston to notify them that they were right and I was wrong. I also included in the letter that I feel like I'm in prison and I'm coming back home, ASAP!

The next day, I received a written telegram from my parents saying that they are so happy to hear that I want to come back home. I began to pack that very same day. I couldn't wait to get out of there. Few hours later, I'm at the bus stop waiting for the bus to come pick me up and take me back to Kingston. On a certain day of the week, the bus carries market vendors to the market place. It so happened to be the same day when I was going home and I wasn't pleased with that. The bus was crowded with market goers; I had such a hard time finding a seat to sit in. There was a bunch of baskets with all types of fruits such as tangerine, ripe bananas, oranges, pineapples, sugar canes, etc., in the passage way and some were on the seats as well. Eventually someone saw that I was looking for a seat and they offered me to sit next to them and another person, so I would have to squeeze up next to them because the space was limited and there should only be two people per seat. Although the ride back to my home was uncomfortable, I was still happy that I was on my way there.

When I finally arrived in Kingston, my parents were waiting for me at the bus stop and there was a taxi already there to take us home. Now we have arrived at our home, and I couldn't have been any more excited to be home again.

CHAPTER 3

Church Day

By the age of sixteen years old, my parents enrolled me into a new school because I was no longer living in St. Mary, and I began classes right away. It was basically a new beginning for me, I began to meet different people at the school and eventually we became good friends. We would meet up before school, during lunchtime, and also after school. At this age, I was discovering a lot about myself. I began dressing differently. I also began wearing make-up because I noticed that at the age of sixteen most girls that I saw at my school wore makeup. I didn't want to be seen as a little girl anymore, I wanted to be seen as a young lady.

As my siblings and I got older, I noticed that my brothers became Christians, but I wasn't really heading that direction. For some reason, I was just not drawn into it at the time. Sunday was my least favorite day because it was the day when my family and I would put aside everything else to go to church. I mean on this day nothing else matters but church. I was basically forced by my parents to go to church.

During church, I sat down in the pew observing all that was taking place around me in the service. Everybody was either jumping up and down, clapping their hands and singing, or wrapped up and caught up in the Holy Spirit, and speaking in tongues. At this point, I would be very anxious to get out of there. My mom would come over, tap me on the shoulder, and say, "Rosie, get up, lift up your hands, and praise the Lord." I would then laugh and say, "Okay, mom." So immediately, I would rise up out of my seat and begin to clap my hands, although I was not really feeling it, but I would rather do that then hear my mother give me the long lecture about the importance of worshiping in church.

It was nothing like hearing the pastor call for offering and tithes, the moment I heard that, I knew that the service was coming to a short end. The preacher preached his heart out. I can't honestly tell you that I remembered everything that he said. But one thing I can say the words that were being spoken out of his mouth was surely getting the people in the church pretty hyped. Usually after church, my mother cooks a big dinner for the family. The whole family would come over and we would eat and spend time together. After the day is well spent everyone would return home, and my mom and I would stay in the kitchen and clean up. I washed the dishes and she washed the pots. We worked as a team to get the kitchen cleaned up as quickly as possible so we could go to bed. After we were finished cleaning, I said goodnight to my mother and gave her a kiss.

CHAPTER 4

Party Time

My alarm clock rang. I didn't know 6 a.m. could come so quick, it's almost as if I just fell asleep, boy, I wanted to sleep a little bit longer, but I knew that it was time for me to get up and get ready for school. I couldn't be late. On the weekdays before going to school, I would meet up with my friends by their homes early in the morning and we would walk together to school and have breakfast in the cafeteria. Usually on a Saturday, my friends and I would just hang out at my house, but this Saturday we wanted to do something a little different. My best friend was introducing me and one of her other friends to a party located on Red Hills Road.

The way my friend was describing this particular party got me really excited and honestly I'm not much of a partygoer, but I was willing to go to the party and check it out to see if it was as good as she made it sound. The only problem for me in this case is that my father is very strict and he does not allow my siblings and me to go out in the nighttime, especially me since I was his baby girl, so he was more overprotective with me. My father works at night and he works for Jamaica Airline, so this was a perfect opportunity for me to sneak out with my friends to go to the party.

I called my friend and told her what I planned on doing and we agreed to go. Saturday came and I got up out of my bed and started my day. I decided that I was going to prepare my outfit ahead of time so it wouldn't be such a hassle for me to sneak out in the night to go to the party. Throughout the day, I was on my best behavior and I helped with the chores to kill sometime. My mom usually goes to bed around 8 p.m., but I waited until around 9 p.m. to get ready and headed out around 9:30 p.m. after double-checking to see if my mom was sleeping.

I walked over to my best friend's house to meet up with her and some of our other friends. Since we didn't have a car, she called a cab for us. Around 10 p.m., the cab picked us up and drove us close to the location where the party was. We had to pay extra cash for every mile the taxi driver drove and we were trying to avoid that so we had the taxi driver drop us off close by the party and we walked the rest of the way. We arrived at the party and I must say my friends and I had eyes staring at us from every direction. It felt like we were celebrities for that night because we were getting so many compliments from people. I must admit it did feel pretty nice.

The music was really loud. Everyone was looking extremely nice, there were food and drinks, such as beer, wine, and rum punch. Almost everybody at the party were dancing, some were drunk, eventually my best friend said to me, "Girl, there are so many good looking boys at this party and one of them needs to come and ask me to dance." All of a sudden, two boys came over to where my friend and I were standing.

The two boys began to compliment us both and finally asked us if we would like to dance with them. We didn't hesitate to say yes. Tonight is the best night ever! My friends and I got home at around 2:30 a.m. I never thought I would be out this late. The latest I have ever been out was until 10 p.m. Well I'm glad I left my window open just in case. I was trying to sneak in as quietly as possible because I didn't want to wake up my neighbors or my mom. Finally, I changed out of my party clothes, went straight into my bed, and fell asleep.

CHAPTER 5

My Father's Death

Sunday morning came by pretty quickly. My mom came in my room and woke me up. She said, "Young lady, you forgot you have church this morning? You need to wake up and get ready right now." So I jumped out of the bed and quickly threw on one of my long church dresses, grabbed my bible, and headed out with my mom.

During the church service, I was in my own zone but I was still listening just a little bit as the preacher was preaching about giving your life to Jesus. Finally, it was 12 p.m., the time that church ended and it was time to go home. I couldn't have been any more excited. When I got home, I changed and went into my bed to get my afternoon nap, because I was still tired. So there I am lying in my bed just thinking about the church service. I just could never understand how people spoke in tongues and got into the Holy Spirit, it's unusual yet it's so amazing. I always wondered to myself every now and then if something like that could ever happen to me.

I finally fell asleep, and all of a sudden, I had this amazing encounter with an angel. In church, I always heard the pastor and even my mother talk about angels, but I always thought that it was just a story. I never really believed it at the time until I experienced it for myself. In this dream that I had, an angel with large white wings came down in my home so powerfully and then he stayed for a little while and flew back up through the roof.

I did not share the dream with anyone because I didn't know how they would take it. I even noticed after that experience when I said something it would happen, but I didn't take it too seriously. When that took place, couple months after that, I moved to a new location with my family. Three years after my family and I moved from the previous location, my father became ill. My family and I had to take him back and forth to the hospital. He had many complaints such as shortness of breath and it began to affect his health tremendously. The doctor told him that he will have to take medication for the rest of his life. Every week we took my father to the hospital. It became a very repetitive task after a while. I was wondering to myself if my father would ever get better. I was tired of him going back and forth to the hospital, and sadly, at the same time he was still working extra hours at the airport.

Almost every night when my father would go to work, he would call us to notify us that he's going to be taking a cab home because he's not feeling well and when he came home, he was always out of breath. I felt so sorry for my father and what he was going through. I wanted to help him but I didn't know how. My father could not sleep in the bed, he had to stand up and lean on something to sleep. Sometimes he had to wake up and walk around, and while he was walking, he would drag his foot and groan. He could not sleep properly, so half the time he did not get a good night rest. Most of the mornings, he's tired and he's cranky.

After a while, my father's complications were getting worst and eventually he had to take a bunch of different medications to help reduce the complication, until one day he went to the hospital and never returned home. The doctor gave us the most devastating news that my father passed away. I couldn't believe what I was hearing. I busted out in tears and began cry out.

I said, "No, this can't be happening. Why so soon?"

Everyone began to cry as well, this day was such a depressing day. A week later, we had to prepare for the funeral. But before the day of the funeral, I remember when I was sleeping I had a weird dream that my father was walking down the hallway of our house and he was making the same groaning sound that he made when he was alive. When I heard it, I immediately covered my ears in the dream, and then suddenly I didn't hear it anymore.

The following morning when I woke up, I told my mother about the dream that I had about my father. But my mother wasn't taking me seriously. Sometimes you think that a person will live forever until one day you see them no more and you have to say goodbye forever. After my father's death, my mom became very quiet.

CHAPTER 6

The Birth of My First Child

Several years passed after my father's death, and things slowly began to fall back in place, but of course, it was not the same like before, because now my dad is gone. Eventually my mom moved out to go live with my older sister, and my other sister and I eventually moved out to live on our own. My other two brothers went their separate ways. The family basically separated after the death of my father.

At age twenty-four, I met a nice young man and we kicked it off, and we fell in love. I was so excited when I first met him, staring into his big bright eyes, I could see our future together. So after a while I moved in with him and eventually I got pregnant with my first child, a girl, and she brightened up our world the day she was born. Her beautiful glistening eyes and her cute little smile made us so happy to be parents.

One night after tucking in my daughter for bed, I took a shower and prepared myself to go to sleep. I went into my bed and relaxed a little until my daughter's father came home from work. All of a sudden, I fell asleep and I received a dream about a throne. In the dream, I was on the rooftop of my home looking up and all of sudden a big white throne came down very close to where I was, I also saw two angels, one to the left and one to right of the throne.

In the dream, it appeared as if there is someone sitting on the throne. Everything in this dream appeared so large, I knew for a fact in my heart that this was the glory of God that came down. But as soon as I took my eyes off the presence of God, I then looked down before me, and all I could see was people running up and down, more like as if they were running away from something. I didn't know exactly what they were running away from, but I could see the expression of fear on their face.

As this took place I was thinking if only they could see what I was seeing up above, then maybe they would not be so afraid. This dream had to be definitely coming from the Lord. Sometimes the Lord shows us signs and wonders to prepare us for a work. Honestly, at the time when I had this dream I really didn't understand the significance of it.

According to Isaiah 6:1-2, Isaiah encountered a similar experience and he said, "That in the year that King Uzziah died, I saw the Lord sitting on a throne, high and lifted up, and the train of his robe filled the temple. Above it stood seraphim; each one had six wings: with two he covered his face, with two covered his feet, and with two he flew." After this night, I never had dreams like this again. I had regular dreams but not like the ones where I see angels and the throne of God.

CHAPTER 7

Moving to the US

My mother went to the US and decided to live in Delaware. She filed for my siblings and me. By the year 1995, the year that my second daughter is born, we moved to the United States and stayed in Delaware. This was such a grand opportunity for my family and me because we always wanted to live a better life and have better jobs. I was definitely looking forward to a new beginning.

After a few years living in the United States, I realized that it surely was not a bed of roses as people perceived it to be. My children's father and I eventually got married and I had my third child. At first, everything seemed to be good between him and me. But I feel like America can either change people for the best or the worst. Well, in my case, it changed my husband for the worst. After my third child with him, he wasn't the same. He took freedom to a whole new level, meaning he was not doing his share in his responsibilities.

Sadly, even though I was married, I felt completely alone in everything because my husband wasn't working. I was doing almost everything by myself, such as paying the bills, taking care of the home, and taking care of the children. The only good thing is that when I went to work he was home with the kids so at least I didn't have to hire a babysitter. I finally took the courage and confronted my husband and told him how I was feeling and he listened to me and we tried to work together to come up with a different plan. He told me about some great job opportunities that would benefit us as a family, and most of these job opportunities are located in Florida.

He then mentioned that it would be best if we would move to Florida. I agreed with him to move to Florida. I couldn't really deal with the cold weather any longer because I had to wake up around 5 a.m. almost every morning to go to work and I would have to leave from one job to the next and I would come home with a cold. This eventually affected my health, so I did not mind moving more down south.

We finally made the decision to move down to Florida. We didn't have much to bring with us. Since we were driving down there, we tried to pack a limited amount of stuff. It's almost as if we were starting all over again. We drove all the way down to Florida and I must say I did enjoy the long journey. We did get lost a couple of times but we did find our way in the long run, so it wasn't too bad. We finally arrived at the beautiful sunshine state!

CHAPTER 8

Moving to Florida

I must say Florida's scenery is beautiful. I felt like I was back in Jamaica. So the moment we moved down here, my husband and I were ready to get our lives up and going. Of course going job hunting and finding somewhere to live was first priority. Thank God, my husband and I have relatives that lived there. So we decided to stay with our relatives for a little while until we got on our feet. My family there was very supportive and understanding toward our situation. My husband's sister would always give us money and clothes for our kids. Months later, my husband and I were able to find a two-bedroom apartment in a decent location, which was pretty affordable for us at the time.

We lived in there for a year. My husband got a job so he could help out with the bills and our kids. Everything was going so good until one day I began to notice some changes with my husband, mainly in his communication with me. I noticed he would come home really late and sometimes he didn't call me to let me know what's going on. Usually he would come home before dinnertime and if he is running late or something comes up unexpectedly at work he would still try to get in touch with me and give me a heads up about what he's doing.

Couple months after that, I noticed even some changes in our finances. He wasn't contributing financially like he said he was going to. He got a job now, so what's the problem? We would split up the bills, he would pay some and I would pay for some. Now all of a sudden my phone is being blown up by bill collectors, saying that they're giving me a final notice. After all, the bills needed to get paid so of course I had no other choice, but to pay for the bill and ask questions later.

Sometimes, I had to even use my debit card and get an overdraft because I didn't have enough money to cover everything. Most of the times, I ended up being broke. I thought to myself what in the world is going on. I had to get to the bottom of this and speak to my husband about it. So one day I pulled my husband aside and asked him, "What is going on?" He didn't know what to say when I asked him this particular question. Eventually he stopped helping me and moved out. The last words he told me when moving out is that he took care of the kids long enough and he doesn't want to do it anymore.

Although hearing those words that came out of his mouth broke my heart dearly, it was my children that I felt sad for the most. I mean they didn't deserve this at all. I thought to myself, *How can a father say that he has taken care of his children long enough and he can't do it anymore?* But this is my life story. Even though I was hurting deep within, I had to stay strong for my children. I delivered the disturbing news to my oldest daughter because I felt like she would understand. Sadly, I didn't know that she was keeping a big secret from me. She kept this secret from me since we were living in Delaware. Apparently, her father told her not to tell me anything or else…

So after I delivered the news to her about what her father said, she began to cry and said, "Mom, I have to tell you something very important."

Then I said, "What is it, honey?"

She continues, "Well, mom, dad told me not to tell you this but I can't keep it in any longer, I can't act as everything was always perfect. Please forgive me, but dad was involved with another woman behind your back."

I was extremely surprised to hear this when my daughter told me this.

"Sweetie, why didn't you tell me? All these years and you kept this from me?"

My daughter began to apologize and explained to me that she was afraid of what her dad would do to her if she had said something. I could only imagine how my daughter felt. A part of me felt highly disappointed in her and another part of me felt sorry for her. I had to make up my mind, put all of this behind me, and move forward.

To women out there who are going through a storm in their relationships, whether it's with their spouse or children, or struggling to make two ends meet, I just want to let you know that it's okay, you know why because I understand. My husband cheated on me and he left me all alone with three kids. Can you imagine how devastating that was for me? Can you imagine how disappointed I was? But this is why I can confidently encourage you and tell you that it's okay, because this experience made me a stronger woman and if it made me stronger as a person then it will also make you stronger. Because I overcame with the help of Jesus then you will overcome too. Remember that with God all things are possible. If you trust in the Lord and let him in, he will give you his joy and peace.

Everyone's healing process is different but what matters the most is that you are healed. Whatever you can do to help yourself I say do it and do it right away. First of all, seek God or seek counseling. Try your hardest to move on and forget the pain of yesterday. If I didn't motivate myself to move forward, my sadness would have surely turned into depression. Sometimes you have to encourage yourself even if you have someone encouraging you already. You have to know your own value and your worth before the eyes of God, because you're not going to always have people around to encourage you. Sometimes the people that you need the most when you're in a tough spot are nowhere to be found. So get into the habit of being a self-motivator.

CHAPTER 9

Left Alone

After a few months, my children's father came back to the apartment unexpectedly. I thought that I wasn't going to see him anymore after that day he moved out. I guess probably he felt guilty. He told me he would visit the kids every day of the week but he would not live with us anymore. When I heard that, I thought he was going to help take care of the kids financially. Eventually every day of the week became once a week, until one day he just stopped visiting altogether. He still didn't give me any money for the kids, for crying out loud, I didn't even have a number to call him so that the kids could stay in touch. When he made phone calls, he always called using a blocked number or call box. So now I was officially on my own as sad as it is to say, I had no one to turn to.

I never felt so alone like the way I felt at that moment. I continuously said to myself, "*Why me? What did I do wrong? Wasn't I a good wife?*" With these questions I asked myself, I felt like depression was coming upon me. So I wasn't thinking as clearly as I should. I felt like I was in bondage and I needed to be set free. I didn't want to feel sad anymore, I didn't want to feel hurt anymore and I no longer wanted to feel neglected. Just when I was forgetting all about what my husband did, he comes and visit out of nowhere and made it seem like he was going to help out, but he didn't. It's not enough to just visit the kids. You have to be concerned about their well-being.

Ladies, I strongly encourage you to be careful on who you have children with. Because some men may seem perfect when you meet them until you marry them and have children with them. Let God choose your husband and if you already do have kids and it's with the wrong man, and the man is a deadbeat, then do your very best to be the best parent that you can be for your children. Love them, sacrifice for them, encourage them, and also set an example for them. Most importantly give your life to the Lord if you haven't already and begin to pray for your children and teach them to love God. The word of God says, according to Proverbs 22:6, "train a child in the way he should, and when he is old he will not depart from it."

One day, I was walking in my complex where I lived when I saw a lady, who apparently injured her foot, and I went over to assist her. I gave her a ride in my car and drove her to where she lived. After that, we exchanged our names and numbers and then I left and went home. After two weeks, the lady that I helped gave me a phone call. Even though I was living in Florida for almost a year, I didn't know anyone besides my family. I never really got out like that. So I answered and we spoke a little bit and she was asking me how long have I been living here.

I responded, "I've been living here for a year," then I said, "Why do you ask?"

Then she said, "Well I've been living here most of my life and I have never seen you before."

Then I said, "Oh, I moved here not too long ago."

Shortly after that, we became good friends. She called me up and checked up on me and eventually I got out of my shell and began to call her to see how she was doing. You know it felt good to have someone else to talk to besides my children. One day my friend called me up and asked me if I would like to go out for lunch with her. Of course, when she asked me this, I was jumping for joy on the inside. I said to myself, *"I'm being invited to go somewhere? I mean me? This is great!"* Immediately, I told her yes.

"I was hoping you would say that," she replied. "I'll be over there in twenty minutes, so be ready then," she said.

As soon as I got off the phone with her, I jumped into the shower and I got myself ready right away. I didn't really have that much nice clothes, most of my clothes were winter clothes because I lived up north originally and I haven't shopped since I came down to Florida. So I just wore what I had, and plus, I don't think it really matters what I'm wearing to go out to lunch as long as I looked decent. Finally, my friend Sandra called to let me know that she was outside. I grabbed my purse and went outside to meet her.

"Hey, Sandra, how are you?"

"Hey, Rose, I'm doing pretty well, are you ready to go?"

"Yes, I'm ready," I replied. "So where exactly are we going for lunch?" I asked.

"Well, I would like to take you to the Red Lobsters. It's one of my favorite restaurants and I believe it's going to be your favorite restaurant too."

We arrived at the restaurant and she began ordering lunch for us. I was fine with her choosing for me because I didn't really have a preference when it came to seafood. Shrimp, fish, lobster, crabs, you name it, I enjoyed it. I must admit the restaurant that she took me to is very nice and the customer service is great. I hoped the food tastes as well as it smells. The waitress arrived with our order and we began eating. After a while Sandra began to ask me where I am originally from, what do I like to do for fun, what places I went to since I've been in Florida, etc. I told her that I'm from Jamaica and I like to go out for dinner and I enjoy going out to the beach and I've never really been anywhere since I came down to Florida. She was so shocked when I told her this.

"I have to take you around," she eagerly said.

CHAPTER 10

Finally A Social Life

I went home after lunch and I must admit I really did enjoy myself. It was nice to get out a little. A week later, Sandra called me and asked me if I would like to go to the mall with her. She said that she's going to a party tonight and she wants to buy a nice outfit. Prior to that, she asked me if I would like to come with her to the party. I told her I don't have anything fancy to wear for that occasion. Then she told me not to worry about it, that she will buy an outfit for me.

Can you imagine the thoughts that were going through my head at this moment? Someone actually wanted to spend their money on me. This is unbelievable! She bought lunch for me the other day and now she's going to buy me clothes. This is almost too good to be true. So I quickly got myself together, because I didn't want to keep her waiting when she came.

She came and picked me up then we headed to the mall and she showed me around a little and introduced me to the stores that had fashionable apparel at affordable prices. She told me to choose what I liked and she will pay for it. I asked her if she was sure about this and she said of course. I had a little doubt because I'm used to buying things for myself but since she offered I just took the offer and ignored those doubts that I had.

I looked around the store a little and, what do you know, my eyes were drawn to this drop dead gorgeous dress. This dress was a black mini dress with lace sleeves and sequence details all over.

I immediately grabbed the dress off the rack and showed it to my friend Sandra. When she saw the dress, her mouth dropped open.

"This is beautiful, you are going to look stunning," she said.

I totally agreed with her.

She bought the dress for me and she bought herself a dress too. She invited me over to her apartment, showed me her closet, and told me that I could choose any shoes that I wanted. She had a lot of shoes. Even though she told me to take any shoes I wanted, I could only allow myself to take one pair. I took a pair of red pumps because I thought that it would match my dress perfectly. Sandra then looked at the shoes that I chose and handed me a red purse that matched the shoes.

Around 8 p.m., I went home and got ready for the party. I told my children that I'm leaving and that I will see them later. I asked my mother if she could come over and watch the children for me. My mother lived close by so it wasn't a problem for her to come and stay. Around quarter to 11 p.m., I heard my phone ring and it was Sandra calling to tell me that she was outside and I needed to come now.

Half an hour later, we arrived at the party. We headed into the building, the music was loud, almost everyone was dancing, some were drinking, and others were just sitting down and listening to the music. Sandra immediately grabbed my hand and pulled me to the middle of the floor to dance. Eventually two men came and saw us, and began to dance with us. I was really enjoying myself. Hours passed by and we were still having a good time on the dance floor. The bright lights came on long after that, and the DJ alerted everyone that it was time to go home.

Everyone got themselves together and headed out of the building. Sandra and I on the other hand stayed and talked a little with the two men that came to dance with us. They asked us for our phone numbers and we gave it to them then we headed home after that. It was already three in the morning, I could just feel the sleep coming down on me the moment we entered into the car, I was just glad that I wasn't the one driving. Sandra arrived at my apartment, dropped me off, and headed home.

CHAPTER 11

A New Relationship

Later on during the day, I received a call from the gentleman that I was dancing with last night. I was surprised that he actually called me. We spoke on the phone for about five minutes. He wanted to know if I would like to go out with him tomorrow.

I told him, "I'm not sure. I have to think about it."

After a while he kept blowing up my phone and asking me if I made a decision yet.

I told him, "I'm not interested in getting into a relationship right now because I'm still going through a healing process from my previous relationship, you and I dancing was just for fun, okay."

Then he asked me, "So why did you give me your phone number?"

Then I said, "Well I didn't know you were going to actually call me."

Then he explained to me, "If a beautiful woman gives me her number, of course I'm going to call her."

I laughed when he said that, and then I asked him, "Re-introduce yourself to me, what's your name?"

He was shocked, "Wow, I thought you knew my name, Rose."

"Wow, I see you remember my name," I replied surprised.

"Yes, I could never forget your name. Well, anyway, my name is Mike."

"Okay, Mike, it's very nice to meet you."

"And it's very nice to meet you, Rose."

We spoke on the phone for a little while and then I told him that I had something to do and that I will call him later. Mike seems like a very nice man but I just wasn't sure if I was ready for anything serious. My heart was broken by the father of my children, a man that I thought loved me and would always be there for me and my children. I don't want to rush into anything, but then again, I don't want to be alone. I needed some advice from someone. So I called Sandra and spoke to her about how I was feeling, and she encouraged me and told me to just give Mike a chance and to forget about the past. I thought about what she said, and I said you know what, maybe she's right. What's the least that can happen? If anything happens, I'll just stop talking to him if I see that he's not treating me right.

Mike called me the following day and asked me if I would like to go out to lunch with him and I thought about it for a few seconds and I said, "Okay." He was so happy to hear that.

He responded excitedly, "Okay, great! I will come and get you around 12:30 p.m., by the way where do you live?"

I told him my address and it so happened that he was familiar with the area. After getting off the phone with him, I got ready.

I looked at the time and it was 12:29 p.m. All of a sudden, my phone rang and it was Mike calling me to let me know he's outside. I was impressed that he came on time. It seemed like he was a man of his word. I went outside and went into his car. He asked me before we left where would I like to go for lunch, and I told him Red Lobster. He agreed and we headed out to Red Lobster. We arrived at the restaurant and he told me that I can order anything that I wanted from the menu and I didn't' have to worry about the price. So the moment he said that I grabbed the menu and I looked for the most expensive meal, and also my favorite meal, which was lobster tail, scallops, and shrimps, and I ordered a Strawberry Daiquiri, which was a fruit drink with a little alcohol additive.

The waiter came and took our order, and brought the meal to our table ten minutes after. When the meal arrived, I went straight to eating. During this time, Mike and I got to know each other a little bit better. Few hours after that he took me home and told me he would call me later. I enjoyed Mike's company and I was look-ing forward to seeing him again. Soon after that, Mike and I began dating regularly, and eventually he and I became closer friends. Five months after that on a late Saturday afternoon, I invited Mike over to my home to meet my children. He came over almost every day after that. Some days I would invite him over for dinner. We began a real relationship a month later.

CHAPTER 12

New Beginning

The New Year came and it was time for me to make some changes in my life. I filed for my tax in January and decided I wanted to move into a new house. I was tired of living in this small two-bedroom apartment. Mike and I were still together and I could see a future with him. During the week, I met someone who was telling me about a house for rent and they gave me a number to call for more information. I called and I spoke to the person who was renting out the home and we made a deal. I met with him. I visited the location, looked at the home, and I liked it, so I decided to sign the contract right away.

Around February, my family and I packed up and moved into our new home. We moved into a three-bedroom house with a big backyard full of fruitful trees. This was a new beginning for my family and me. This house that we moved into was so beautiful and the neighborhood was pretty decent and our neighbors were very friendly. Around this time, my mother moved in with us and Mike moved in with us as well.

Everything was finally coming together in my life. I met a good man, I moved into a nice house, and my mother always helped out with my kids when I went to work. This is exactly how I imagined my life being, but sadly, as I am telling you this now, this is not how my life continued to remain. This is where my real life story begins.

Thursday morning while I was driving to work, I felt something unusual come over me. I found myself speaking in tongues. I was speaking during the whole ride until I reached work. This feeling was different and it felt real good, but I didn't understand why this happened so suddenly.

Friday morning when I was driving, the same feeling came over me again and it was powerful and I began to speak in tongues. After that experience, there was a shift in my life. I didn't feel the same anymore. I began to look at things differently. The man I was living with began to look different to me as well. I wondered to myself why am I living with him.

It seemed as if the scales were removed from my eyes. Even so, I continued to live with him, but my feelings for him weren't the same as before. I had a few disturbing dreams few nights after about Mike. Actually, I received the same dream about Mike night after night. I was curious to know what these dreams about Mike signified. I don't know why I keep getting the same dream about him. In the dream that I had, Mike was seen lying in the bed without a shirt on while at the same time standing up with his shirt on and he was talking on the phone to a woman.

I really didn't know what was going on, I was so confused. I remember my mother always told me if I didn't understand something that I'm to pray to God for understanding. So I took the initiative and prayed to God about the repetitive dreams that I had about Mike and the answer I received was that it was time for him to leave. So I told Mike that he and I can't be together anymore, and we can't live together any longer. A week later I noticed that Mike was packing up to move out.

When Mike left, it was like as if a big burden was lifted up. I realized that he was not the man for me. To be honest, I was happy, I felt so free, and from that day I decided to go to church. I started to visit a community church and I was baptized and filled with the Holy Ghost.

God knows how to get his children's attention. Sometimes he will allow you to feel his presence unexpectedly, just like what happened to me when I was on my way to work. I mean this feeling of empowerment came over me out of nowhere, and I honestly don't know how it happened but all I know is that the Lord revealed himself to me. Speaking in tongues is nothing to be ashamed of because that's the way we communicate with God; it's the heavenly language. When the Lord begins to empower you, he changes your perspective about life, actually about everything, and honestly, when I experienced the Lord's touch, I just didn't feel the same and I felt the need to give my life to Jesus. I came home and the man that I was once crazy about all of sudden just didn't look the same to me anymore. When we are in our flesh we are after the desires of the flesh and only seek to do the will of the flesh. But when we give our life to Jesus, we want to die to the fleshly desires and seek the will of the Lord.

By communicating with me through a dream, the Lord told me that he did not want me to be with Mike anymore and that he doesn't want him living in my home. To some people it might seem strange, but it was God's will and I had to obey. Sometimes we may think someone is for us, but what does God think? What God thinks is what matters the most, because he knows his children and he knows every thought and every deep secret. So God had his reason for why he did not want this man in my life anymore and I am perfectly fine with that.

CHAPTER 13

Giving My Life to Jesus

The moment I gave my life to Christ, I entered into a new beginning. Giving my life to Christ was the best decision that I have ever made. My dreams were becoming more spiritual and I was going into a deeper realm with the Lord. For example, there was one dream that I received ten years ago when I was in Jamaica. In the dream, it appeared as if there was someone sitting on the throne.

Everything in this dream appeared so large. Also, as soon as I took my eyes off the presence of God, I then looked down before me, and all I could see was people running up and down with the expression of fear on their faces. I never forgot this dream and I recently received a similar dream like it. In this dream that I received recently there was someone sitting on the throne and this time I saw the person wearing a crown on his head and he wore a white robe, I believe strongly in my heart that this person was the Lord.

The following night I received another dream, and in the dream I was looking up in the sky and I saw a large screen in the sky. What appeared on the large screen was a tall man, after that he disappeared. Afterward, a lady came out and she began to dance and then she disappeared. Finally someone else came out. I could see the top portion of their body and I noticed that there was a bright light shining around their head. This person also had medium-length dark brown hair, and this person was revealed to me in the dream by the Holy Spirit as being Jesus.

When I looked up in the sky to the right side, I saw a cross formed out of the clouds and someone was on the cross, but I didn't see the details up close. After I woke up out of the dream, I prayed to the Lord to show me who was on the cross. Four days after, I received another dream that my sister and I were outside running toward my home and I was shouting, "When the trumpet sound," and I continued to repeat those words. Outside appeared so dark, as if it was going to rain. The breeze was blowing so heavily and it felt like a disaster was about to prevail.

We entered into my home and I could see the curtain blowing up by the heavy breeze, I then told my sister to close the curtain and she refused to do it, so I got up and did it myself. As I was about to close the curtain, I saw Jesus behind the curtain with the crown that was made out of thorns around his head, he also had the nails in his feet and in his wrist. The Lord answered my prayer and revealed himself to me in this dream to let me know that it was him on the cross. When I woke up from my slumber, warm tears came running down my face and immediately I began to praise the Lord. At this moment, I'm even more convinced than ever before that the Lord almighty God is real in my life. According to Psalms 21:2, the word of God mentions that, "Thou hast given him his heart's desire, and hast not withhold the request of his lips."

Children of God, don't take dreams lightly because, believe it or not, God communicates with his children through dreams and visions. It's always best to keep a journal or a notepad along with a pen on your bed side so that you can record your dreams when you wake up from your sleep. God also gives us directions through dreams and visions. For example, in Matthew 1:20, the angel of the Lord appeared unto Joseph in a dream saying, "Joseph, thou son of David, fear not to take unto thee Mary thy wife; for that which is conceived in her is of the Holy Ghost." Also, verse 24 mentions that after Joseph was raised from his sleep he did as the angel of the Lord had bidden him. See Matthew 2:12-23 for more about God's directions given out in dreams.

CHAPTER 14

Angelic Visitation

I went through a season in my life where I was receiving spiritual dreams periodically. I remember one afternoon I felt a sharp pain on the right side of my stomach and I decided to go lay down in my bed. Momentarily after I fell asleep that same afternoon I received a dream. My daughter was in this dream and in it she came and lay right next to me, then she began to touch the right side of my stomach where the pain was.

After I woke up I still felt the pain, but I noticed later on when I went to work that night that I didn't feel the pain anymore. Instantly I remembered the dream that I had earlier this afternoon and I thought to myself what if God sent someone to heal my stomach. I feel strongly in my spirit that I received a visitation from an angel. In Psalms 91:11, the word of God says the "Lord shall give his angels charge over me to keep me in all my ways."

All these things that were happening to me was so unusual, I needed someone to talk to and of course not just any ordinary person but someone who was knowledgeable about dreams and the spiritual things of God. One evening when I went to work, one of my co-workers came up to me excitedly and gave me a hug, and began to tell me about a church that she recently visited and how the pastor of the church prophesied to her and told her things about her life and what God has in store for her.

I was astonished to hear this so I asked her when she is visiting again. She immediately told me that she was visiting next Friday and she wanted to invite me to come with her on that day. She said she will pick me up and we will go together. Friday came and my co-worker picked me up at around 7:30 p.m. because service began at 8 p.m. sharp. A half hour later, we arrived and we headed into the building where the service was being held. As soon as we walked in, everyone was already praising and worshiping God.

After a while, the pastor of the church came up to the podium, greeted everyone, and welcomed the visitors. She asked for all those that are visiting for the first time to stand up and introduce themselves. Eventually it was my turn to stand up and introduce myself. I told everyone my name and I gave a short testimony. All of a sudden, the pastor looked at me and began to speak into my life.

She said to me, "Woman of God, do you know that you are a chosen vessel of God and God has placed within you a prophetic anointing?"

I could never forget those words that she spoke over me.

She said, "Woman of God, God has given you a work to do for him here on the face of this earth and a time is going to come when God is going stir up the gift inside of you and bring it to manifestation."

I immediately began to lift up my hands and praise God. I couldn't believe what I was hearing. All of my life I always wondered why I am always alone, why my friends are always turning their back on me, why I felt so different from everyone else. After a while my friendship with Sandra didn't last. All of a sudden, she stopped talking to me, she didn't call me anymore. But now I have a clearer understanding of why I felt this way. The prophetess opened up my understanding. Jesus did not go through an easy time when he was here on this earth and because I am one of his that only means that I'm going to go through persecution for his sake.

The pastor told me that I needed to be around people who have the gift and that I'm more than welcome to visit her ministry as long as I wanted to. This was definitely a door being opened for me because I remember asking the Lord in prayer to bless me with someone who is knowledgeable about the spiritual things of God.

CHAPTER 15

Spiritual Transitioning

When I went home that night, I thought deeply about everything the prophetess said to me and I did not take one word that she spoke out of her mouth lightly. I was so excited about doing a work for God. So I decided that I'm going to attend this church that my co-worker invited me to. One night I was sleeping and something unusual took place that night. For some reason I felt a strong force holding me down in my sleep and I was trying to move and call out for help but I felt paralyzed.

When I woke up, I was so terrified, and I felt so weak and drained, as if something or someone came and took all my energy away. I had a challenging time going back to sleep because I was so afraid of what would happen. I wasn't quite sure what was going on but I knew for a fact that this was not normal. I went through this experience for numerous occasions, only the mercy of God sustained me. At times, I felt like I was gasping for air.

On the following morning, I received a phone call from Susan, a lady that I knew from church. She asked me if I would like to come with her tonight to a prayer meeting, to help pray for a woman who is going through trials and temptation in her home, this woman was also experiencing tremendous warfare in her life. I explained to her that this is all new to me but I will go with her. She then told me that this will be a learning experience for me and that I should pay close attention.

At 8 p.m. that night, I arrived at the woman's house for the prayer meeting. I decided to wait for Susan in the parking lot so we could go inside the home together. Suddenly my phone rang and it was Susan calling me to tell me that she won't be able make it to the prayer meeting because something unexpectedly came up on her end and she has to take care of it right away. Now I was contemplating on whether I should go home or stay and pray with the other people that came. I finally made up my mind to stay because I was already there.

I went inside and greeted everyone. We held hands and began to pray for the woman. After we prayed, there was a miraculous shift in the atmosphere. The woman began to break out in tears and gave the Lord thanks for what he has done. I left her house at around one o'clock in the morning and it took about twenty-five to thirty minutes to reach home. I finally arrived home and as soon as I got home, I changed and went to bed by 2 a.m. and I immediately fell asleep.

During the time I was sleeping, I felt a strange presence over me and all I could hear was a bunch of whispering at the windows of my room. I was trying so hard to wake up but the force was very strong so it was difficult for me to open my eyes to see what was going on. I tried to open my mouth to call upon Jesus but it seemed as if the force was trying to keep my mouth shut. I knew that I was calling upon Jesus in my heart. When I was finally able to open my mouth and call out on Jesus in the spirit, I began to say, "Jesus, Jesus, where are you!"

Suddenly, I saw someone with a white veil over their head and they were in full white and carried a rod in their hand. I noticed that there were some white stones at first but then when I looked a little closer it appeared as sheep. When I woke up from my slumber, I felt a sense of joy and peace. I remember reading in the bible that Jesus came to give us peace, not the world's peace, but his peace.

When you are a follower of Christ, sometimes the devil will try to find ways to torment you and make you feel like God is not with you. Keep in mind, according to Psalms 37:39-40, remember "the salvation of the righteous is of the Lord: he is their strength in the times of trouble. And the Lord shall help them and deliver them: he shall deliver them from the wicked, and save them because they trust in him." The Lord will not leave you nor forsake you. The moment you cry out for help the Lord will be there to rescue you.

CHAPTER 16

The Glory of God

Saturday morning as I woke up from my sleep I saw the glory of God come down in my home with a bright light and within the bright light, I noticed that there was a white cloud. In a short moment the glory of the Lord disappeared. The Lord can show his children anything he wants, and he can bring you as deep as you want to go. There is no limit to what God can do in your life. I love the Lord so much and I was extremely hungry and thirsty for his righteousness. Most of all, I wanted to know him on a more intimate level. I wanted to pursue God more. I didn't want to only know God from a religious percept but I wanted to have a personal relationship with him.

Have you ever been in a place in your life where you were tired of hearing your own voice during your personal time with the Lord? Sometimes I found myself praying to the Lord in my secret place but never really taking some time to sit down in silence and hear what he had to say. I just wanted to hear the Lord's voice just like the prophets or the great men of God in the bible did. I took the initiative and began to pray to the Lord.

I said to the Lord, "Come close to me and let me hear your voice."

I remember before I fell asleep I prayed to hear the Lord's voice, and I remember hearing his voice that same night.

I dare you to try it for yourself if you haven't already. Get out of your comfort zone and pray to God to hear his voice and see what happens. Soon after that, you're going to be having a conversation with God and that's when the real relationship develops. The Lord has revealed himself and his power to me in so many wonderful ways. I can testify about the miraculous experiences that occurred in my life. The Lord always provided a solution to my problems when I least expected, like this one I'm going to share with you.

I've been having back pain for years and I think it's because of my cheap old uncomfortable mattress that I had since I've lived in my old apartment. Sadly, I never bought a new one since then. I prayed to the Lord to bless me with a new mattress and as I was praying to the Lord immediately he showed me a new mattress, it looked so real it was almost as if I could physically touch it. Eventually God blessed me with the money to purchase a brand new mattress.

A month later, after sleeping on my new mattress, I noticed that I would wake up with red marks on my arm and often times I found myself itching all over. This happened almost every night when I woke up. I can't believe that this is happening, I just bought the mattress for crying out loud.

Early Saturday morning I woke up and did some laundry. I took all the sheets off the bed and put them in the washer. When I came back into my bedroom to put new sheets on the bed I notice that there was what seemed to look like black spots in the creases around the mattress. I decided to take a closer look and as I looked a little closer, I noticed that the black spots weren't actually spots but they were bed bugs. I was so shocked when I saw this. I don't even know how I'm going to get rid of them. Before going to sleep that night, I prayed to the Lord and the Lord showed me duct tape taped all around the mattress. Before you know it, I bought some duct tape the following morning and I taped it around the creases of the bed. When it was time for me to go to sleep, I can honestly say that I slept peacefully and I woke up with no red marks or itching. Praise God!

Couple days after that, I took the tape off and the bed bugs were all dead. I looked around the bed to see if there were any more bugs, I even looked under the mattress and I didn't see any. Every day, I made it a point of duty to examine my bed thoroughly to make sure the bed bugs were actually gone and they're gone. I haven't seen one since that day. I took this experience as a blessing from the Lord and

I thank him so much for giving me a solution. The word of God says, "Ask and ye shall receive." His words are true and his words are proven in my life every day.

My life consists of prayer. Prayer is my daily bread. I can't go through my day or begin my day without praying. On Thursday night as I was praying I could see Jesus standing at a gate wearing full white and he told me to come and follow him. My response to the Lord was, "Yes, I will follow." This was a prime example that occurred to me, that when Jesus told his disciples to come and follow him, they dropped everything they were doing and went to go follow Jesus. The Lord is revealing himself more and more to me each day and I want to follow him for the rest of my life.

The Holy Spirit reminded me that I won't always receive support in the decisions I make to follow Jesus. Following Jesus requires our outmost participation such as our obedience, our faith, our worship, and our prayer. It will also require us to give up something to follow him. Those who choose to follow Christ will go through trials and temptation, but the Lord will be there to help us. As it mentions in John 16:3, the Lord says, "These things I have spoken unto you, that ye might have peace. In the world ye shall have tribulation: but be of good cheer; I have overcome the world."

Being a Christ-follower is not always easy but there should never be any regrets. Your friends will sometimes resent you because you no longer do the things that you used to do with them when you were in the world. People will even hate you because you stand up for righteousness and holiness. Jesus said in John 15:18-19, "If the world hates you, you know that it hated me before it hated you. If you were of the world, the world would love his own: but because ye are not of the world but I have chosen you out of the world, therefore the world hateth you."

CHAPTER 17

God Warns Me to Move

I received an insight from the Lord and he told me that he wants me to move and that I had a certain amount of time to pack up and leave. He also warned me that someone was going to break into the house. When I received the insight from God, I was worrying, more like panicking actually because I wasn't prepared. I decided to pack up as much as possible to move out, but at the same time, I still didn't know where I was going. I mean I didn't have any money saved up, the landlord of the home said I owed him $7,000. I was in a tough spot.

I know my Lord doesn't want me to be homeless with my three children, but I felt like I was losing faith. What if I end up being homeless? Maybe that's God's way of testing me. Honestly, I didn't know what to think or believe anymore. What has my life come to? Trial after trial, when is it going to come to an end?

I noticed slowly but surely everything in my home began to fall apart. Mold was forming on top of the ceilings and all over the walls. The fruits in the backyard were drying up. Even insects, bugs, and lizards were infesting the home.

I remember I was getting something from under the dining room table by the kitchen and what do you know, I saw lizards in some of my china dishes that I had packed away in the box. I screamed so loud, I thought *how in the world did these lizards get in here in the first place.* I immediately began to plead the blood of Jesus against them because I had a feeling that this was the work of the enemy, I don't know how exactly but I knew someway somehow this was not coming from God.

The Lord was so right I need to get out of here, and I mean fast. I still have no idea where my children and I are going to stay, but I had to keep my faith and not lose hope. Deep down inside I felt like I was going to give up. But I had to stay strong for my children's sake, because I'm all they have. God will sometimes put you in a place of discomfort to increase your faith in him.

Monday morning arrived and I took my eldest daughter to school. After I dropped her off to school, I returned home. When I entered into my home, the atmosphere didn't feel too right for some reason. I went ahead and did some investigating around the home, I checked the bedrooms to see if everything was okay and it wasn't until I checked my children's bathroom and I noticed that the window near the bathtub area was cracked open. I was so shocked. I couldn't believe what I was seeing, someone broke into the house. It was such a blessing that nothing important was stolen.

Oh my goodness! The Lord did warn me that someone was going to try to break into the home. All I could do at this point was just trust God. So I packed up almost everything that I and my family needed into my vehicle and gave away the things that we didn't have space for such as the furniture. The rest that we didn't have any use for were thrown in the garbage.

I wasn't moving as fast as I should because I had a lot on my plate. I was contemplating on whether I should stay for a few more days or leave right away because I saw a mop in the spirit cleaning out my home. Surprisingly the spirit of God gave me an open vision about someone breaking in the house a second time and he showed me that this time, they are going to break in from the back door and he showed me how they were going to do it. Immediately, I thought *that old devil wants me to stay*. He thought if he showed me the mop cleaning the home, I would consider the idea, and just clean the home and stay.

But God wanted the opposite, the Lord showed me if I don't hasten to leave the premises by now then tomorrow my family and I are going to be in serious trouble. The moment I received that message I hastened my footsteps and rented out a storage room to put all my belongings in, thank God the storage room was affordable. There were some things that I had to leave back in my children's bedroom because it was contaminated with mold and mildew.

I was very grateful that I had a van, because I didn't have any money to rent a U-Haul truck. The van fit a good amount of stuff. The spirit of God showed me a van and I'm glad I obeyed him, because originally I was going to get a car. I must say the Lord knows how to prepare his children, because he blessed me to have this vehicle for a specific reason and I didn't know until now. He saw exactly what was going to take place.

I finally finished packing away our belongings into the storage room and we left the home immediately because I knew if I didn't obey God I would suffer the consequences and I didn't want to put my children through any more distress. As I drove out of the parking area, I looked at the piece of mess I lived in and broke out in tears.

Now it was time for me to figure out where my children and I were going to stay. I prayed to the Lord and asked for some guidance, I explained to him that I didn't have that much money and I'm out of options, and of course God knew that already, but I still had to communicate with my father up in heaven.

At first, I thought to myself that maybe my children and I can sleep in the storage room, and then I decided to seek as God's word instructed me to "seek and ye shall find." I called a few different hotels and one of the representatives that I spoke to on the phone recommended me to a hotel that charged a fixed rate, where one would have to pay the same price on a weekly basis. I know for a fact that you have to pay daily for most hotels.

The gentleman gave me further information about the hotel and where it was located and I went to the hotel right away and checked in. Before I went to the hotel, the Lord showed me in a vision the hotel room. There was only one king size bed in there and my children and I were lying on the bed together. In my mind, I was picturing a room with two beds. I really did end up being in a room with one king size bed, just like I saw in the vision.

Honestly even though I ended up being in a room with a king size bed like the Lord showed me, I couldn't help but to ask the hotel manager if they had a room with two beds in it. The hotel manager took me to an available room with two beds, but I wasn't feeling it. I preferred the previous room I was in before. The Lord chose this room for me and I need to follow instruction.

When God shows you something or gives you specific instructions just obey and save yourself the heartache. Sometimes what we want isn't always what the Lord wants. Whatever the Lord wants for his children works out for the best.

CHAPTER 18

The Lord Provides a New Home

Three months passed since we've been living in the hotel and I felt in my heart that it was time for me to move and find a home for me and my children to live in, either a house or an apartment and nothing too expensive. One Monday morning after dropping my kids off at school, I went out to seek a home. I asked the Lord to lead me and bless me to live somewhere close to my children's school so I wouldn't have to make multiple trips back and forth to take them to school because there was only one vehicle and I was the only driver. Also it would be so much easier on me because sometimes I would come home from work feeling exhausted and I didn't want my kids to be late for school.

I visited a few locations. The first location I visited was extremely expensive, and the second one that I visited had too many rules and regulations and was expensive as well. Finally, I visited another location and I spoke to someone who lived on the property. The person told me that this was a private property and everyone that lives there own their condo. I walked away feeling disappointed. Honestly, it was a nice area that I wouldn't mind if God blessed me to live there and not only that the location was close to my children's school.

I prayed to the Lord and told him that I would love if he could bless me to live there, but if it's not of his will then I completely understand, and I will keep seeking until he leads me to that right place.

I received a vision two weeks after and in the vision, I saw a black microwave on top of a counter. I could also see the apartment and the stairs of the apartment building. At first, I wasn't too sure about the dream that I had. Until one day, I was at the supermarket and I met this gentleman. I asked him out of desperation if he knew anyone who was renting out their home. He had a very strong accent but I was able to understand him. The gentleman told me that he was a realtor and he knew a lady who was renting out her condo. He called the lady and spoke to her for me and the lady said that she has to check my credit first and if my credit is not up to standard then she would have to charge me two months' rent.

The Lord was definitely working things out on my behalf, because the gentleman put in a good word for me and told the lady that he knew me for years and that I'm a good person and I just needed some help financially. Surprisingly, the lady listened to him and told him that she would give a reasonable price. He called me the following afternoon and told me the good news.

He said, "Rose, the landlord said she checked your credit and your credit isn't in good shape but she said she will work with you and will only charge you one months' rent."

I was very happy to hear that and I said, "Okay, that works for me."

I asked him, "When can I see the place?"

He told me that we can set a day and a time to go look at the condo together. I told him that we could meet on a Saturday at 12 p.m. and he agreed.

The moment I got off the phone with him I began to rejoice.

I said to the Lord, "Have your way, let your will be done in my life here on earth as it is in heaven!"

I shared the good news with my children when I went to pick them up from school and they were excited, too. Saturday came and the realtor called to confirm that we were still meeting up at 12 p.m. to go see the condo location. I got ready, my children got ready, and we all went together. I met up with him at a gas station. He drove in front of us and I followed him to the condo location.

We reached the location and, surprisingly, it was the same private property that I had asked the Lord to bless me with if it was his will. I couldn't believe it, the Lord answered my prayer. Finally, the realtor led me and children upstairs to where the condo was located, when we went inside I saw a black microwave on the counter. I immediately remembered the vision that I had recently, and in the vision all I saw was the stairs of an apartment and on the inside, I saw a black microwave on top of a counter. The Lord confirmed with me through a vision by showing me two elements of the apartment: the microwave and the stairs. Because in reality, the condo was located on the third floor and we had to take the stairs. On this special day, the Lord gave me my heart's desire. Nothing is too hard for the Lord. With him, all things are possible and I thank God for that blessing. The Lord is worthy of all praises, no matter what we are going through we can count on the Lord to make it right. Hallelujah!

Eventually my family and I moved into our new home. I took a trip to the rented storage room and I packed everything into the van. I made a few trips back and forth to the storage and finally cleared out everything and signed off. One day at a time, my children and I were packing out clothes, pan, pots, and other miscellaneous items. God blessed me with some free furniture and he also favored to me to receive some that I didn't have to pay much for. My eldest daughter volunteered to do all the interior design. She did a great job organizing the furniture and giving the home a welcoming presentation.

The following Monday after my children went to school my eldest daughter and I were going out on the road to run some errands. But for some reason when it was time for me to start the vehicle, the van was giving me a difficult time to start up. After trying to start it up a few times, it still wouldn't budge, so I had to call my tow truck company to come and transfer my vehicle to my mechanic. My mechanic took a look at the vehicle and he fixed the problem and the van started up momentarily.

Two weeks after that I was taking my daughter to school and as I was heading to her school I had to make a stop at the four-way stoplight because the light was red. When the light turned green, I drove off, but as I was driving off a woman in a vehicle coming from the opposite direction ran the red light and drove into my van. The side of the van was greatly damaged but my daughter and I didn't receive any injuries. God saved us from a tragedy on this day. The cops came and they resolved everything. I could still drive the vehicle, so I drove the vehicle home and took it to my mechanic a couple days after to get it repaired.

CHAPTER 19

The Lord Saves Me from a Car Accident

Few months after, we were in another accident and this time there was more than one vehicle involved. The person crashed into my car and into another person's car. God blessed us that we survived this accident once again. We could have lost our life that day but the Lord came to our rescue! We got the vehicle fixed again for the third time. A month after that I believe in the month of February in the year of 2013, on a Friday, my family and I were on our way to church and as I was driving I saw that the gas tank was halfway empty.

I drove over to a gas station and purchased some gas. As I was getting into the car, I noticed that there was some smoke coming out from under the hood. There was a man close by and I asked him if he could check out the vehicle and find out where the smoke is coming from. He investigated and he told me all it needs is a little water. He took care of that problem for me and I told him thank you.

We were on our way to church and suddenly I saw smoke coming out from the vehicle again. But I was determined to keep driving because I wanted to go to church and we were already running late. Right after that, I began to see fire rise up from under the hood. I quickly turned off the main road and parked the vehicle. My family and I grabbed our belongings and rushed out of the van. The fire got bigger and then the vehicle caught on fire. Someone saw what took place and called 911. A fire truck along with the cops showed up. The fire was immediately put out and the cops took their report. Few minutes after that, the tow truck came and picked up the vehicle.

I called my insurance company and explained to them what happen to my vehicle and they looked into everything. A week after that, I rented a car. I received a check in the mail from my insurance company that same week and I was going to use the check to purchase another vehicle. I just couldn't keep up with the weekly payment anymore so I decided to go and check out some car lots, but all the vehicles there were too expensive.

I went to my mechanic a week later to see if he knew anyone who was selling cars at an affordable price. It so happened that I met a woman who was getting her vehicle fixed there and we were just conversing a little bit and she told me that she sells cars for a living. I told her to give me her card and I will call her.

I called her to set an appointment to see the vehicles that she had. She gave me the time and the location. I drove over to the address that she gave me and I saw a few vehicles there. There was one that caught my attention the most, it was a 2005 dark gray Lexus truck. I used the $6,000 check to purchase the Lexus and the woman put a sold sign on the vehicle so anyone who saw it would know that someone bought it. I told her that I would have to take the bus back over here because I have the rental and I don't have anyone to drive the truck.

She said, "Okay, don't worry, it will still be here when you come."

I looked at the paper work for my Lexus truck and I was able to take it home that day. I was so grateful that God blessed me to have a vehicle that is a little more up to date and not only that he blessed me with the money to purchase it. Five months later, I had a dream that I was driving in the Lexus truck and I met into a car accident. When I woke up, I prayed against it and I left it alone. Prior to that, within two months, I actually figured into the accident that I saw in my dream.

The cops along with the ambulance arrived at the scene and I couldn't really give any specific details in regards to the accident because my head was throbbing and I felt like I was going to pass out.

One of the assistants from the ambulance came over to me, took my blood pressure, and told me that it was above normal, and then the ambulance rushed me to the emergency room. The nurse monitored my blood pressure. After a few hours, it went back to normal and they released me right away. Unfortunately, after I was released from the hospital, I had no other choice but to walk home because I didn't have any money to take the taxi or bus and my phone was dead so I couldn't call anyone for a ride.

As I walked home, I asked the Lord to sustain me because for some reason I began to feel tingling in my hands and in my feet and I came to a realization that I was experiencing a whiplash from the accident. At first, I was going back to the hospital but then I said, you know what, I trust that the Lord will sustain me. It took me almost two hours to reach home and I walked approximately eight miles. When I got home, I felt a sharp pain in my back, so I decided to call the chiropractor the following morning and explained to her the discomfort that I was feeling on my back. She told me to come by the office and she will begin the back treatment.

Later in the afternoon, I went to the office and met with the chiropractor. She took me into a room where there was a bed. She told me to lie on my belly and she applied the treatment to my back. When it was time for me to get off the bed, I had a very challenging time. I felt even more pain in my back than before.

I asked the chiropractor, "What happened? I thought I was going to feel better after the treatment but now I feel worst."

So she made an appointment for me to meet with a back specialist. After meeting with the back specialist, he examined my back and shared with me some disappointing news.

He said, "Rose, unfortunately, according to the test results, your back is in terrible condition and the only way to eliminate this pain permanently is by getting surgery."

I didn't agree with him at all.

I told him, "I'm not going to do it because I believe there is another way and Jesus is the way!"

I continued to attend the chiropractor's sessions. They gave me medication and pain relievers for the back pain but honestly nothing seemed to work. I still had a hard time getting up out of my bed, to bend down was a hassle, and I couldn't stand up for too long.

Monday night, I went to bed and I received a dream that I was attending a church and a prophet called me out of the audience and began to prophesy to me about what's going on with me.

I went to church on a Thursday evening and the prophet called me out and prophesied to me about my back. I didn't tell him anything about myself and what I was going through with my back. He continued to prophesy to me and told me that I got into a car accident, he even went as far as describing the color of the vehicle that I was driving.

Then he told me, "Woman of God, God is going to heal your back tonight and I mean right now! Listen here," he said. "I'm not going to even touch you because God is the one who is going to heal you not me. After this night, there will be no need for you to return to the chiropractor said the Lord almighty God."

Everything the prophet said to me was right on point, which only means that God was speaking to him. That same night, God healed my back and I never felt the same after that night. I was able to bend down and touch my toes without any pain or discomfort. That wasn't something I could do before. The Lord has performed so many great miracles in my life. I just can't stop rejoicing. The Lord is the great physician. He sends out his word and it heals, and healing is the children's bread according to Matthew Chapter 15:22-29. Don't hesitate to call upon the Lord when you are going through sickness or pain in your body because sometimes the doctor can't help you but remember that Jesus is the healer.

CHAPTER 20

The Lord is the Great Physician

Sunday, January 11th, 2015, I was at work taking care of a patient and all of a sudden I had a quick insight and the spirit of the Lord showed me the anatomy of a body and I could see the organs, organ tissues, and all the blood cells. While I was seeing all of this, I heard the Spirit of God say cancer. I thought that the spirit of the Lord was referring to the patient that I was looking after at the time. Immediately I began to pray for the patient. Two weeks after that, I went to church on a Tuesday night when a prophet from out of state was visiting. The prophet called me out and prophesied to me that I had cancer in my right breast. He told me that the Lord is going to heal me tonight and the lump is going to shrink to nothing.

The Holy Spirit also revealed to the prophet that I had four ulcers in my chest area and he laid his hands upon me and prayed over me and the Lord healed me from that as well on the same night.

Even though the right breast was healed, I was still concerned about my left breast. For some reason I had that concern rested upon my heart. But the word of God according to 2 Timothy 1:7 says that the Lord did not give us the spirit of fear but of power, love, and a sound mind. So even though I was having a major concern about that issue I didn't want my concern to turn into fear. When the service was finished, I went into my car and I began speak to the

Lord about my concern and asked him if he could show me a healing scripture.

Momentarily after that I opened my bible and surprisingly I opened to Isaiah chapter 53 verse 5, it was such a blessing I didn't have to turn the pages, I just landed right on that scripture. As I read Isaiah 53:5 I noticed that the word of God said, "But he was wounded for our transgressions, he was bruised for our iniquities: the chastisement of our peace was upon him; and with his stripes we are healed." Bingo, that's what I needed to hear! By his stripes I am healed, I declared and decreed. I thanked the Lord for leading me to that scripture because I needed assurance.

There's a church that I visit frequently and a lot of the guest speakers who come to minister are prophetic women and men of God. In April 2015 I received a letter from the pastor of the church that I visit regularly informing me about an anointing woman of God that was going to be a guest speaker at his church and he was inviting me to attend. I took a quick look at the photo of the guest speaker that was coming to the church and I received a vision from the Lord. In the vision, I saw the woman who was going to speak at the church lying in the hospital bed and there was another lady witnessing to her. The lady in the vision told the woman of God that she is healed and to receive her healing in the name of Jesus.

The guest speaker was going to speak on a Tuesday night in the month of April and it was such a blessing that I would be able to attend her service because Tuesday is my usual day off. I was excited that I was going to be able to share with her the wonderful good news that the Lord has imparted into my spirit about her healing even though I never met her before. This will be the first time that I will actually see her in person.

I went to the service Tuesday night and when it was offering time I got up, gave my offering, and took this time as an opportunity to tell the woman of God what the Lord showed me in a vision about her healing. When I shared the good news with her about her healing, she was so delighted and she said to me that she receives it. Thursday night, I attended church and the Prophetess was testifying about her healing and on what the Lord delivered her from. I immediately remembered what the Lord shared with me about her and I said to myself that's a confirmation. God is good!

After she testified, she was led to call out individuals from out of the pew and prophesy to them. I was one of those individuals that she called out from the pew. When she called me out, she prophesied to me about my left breast having cancer but she told me that the Lord said I am healed and I felt more affirmation when I received my healing this time. The Lord is a miracle worker and I thank him so much for not only hearing my prayer but delivering me from sicknesses and diseases. As it is said in Romans 2:11, "For there is no respect of persons with God." The same thing he did for me, he can do for you if you just believe.

What I shared with you about my life is the truth and it is my desire that women like myself who are single, sick, or broken will experience the love of God like I did. And, don't worry, men, I didn't forget about you, stay encouraged and don't grow weary in doing well because in your due season the Lord will lift you up. Remember, God is a faithful god and he will not let his children down. He's here for us through good times and desperate times. He is our present help in the times of trouble. Psalms 34:6 says that the poor man cried and the Lord heard him, and saved him out of all his troubles. This verse is a reminder to those who may feel like God has not seen their tears or heard their prayer. If God delivered the poor man from all his troubles, then why wouldn't he be able to deliver you from yours?

Through my testing and trials, I had to encourage myself with the word of God and I had to continuously remind myself about what the Lord has said and done for me. I know that I wouldn't be the woman that I am today if I didn't have the word of God. I know I wouldn't have been able to share my story if it wasn't with the help of the Lord. James 1:12 says, "Blessed is the man that endures temptation: for when he is tried, he shall receive the crown of life which the Lord hath promised to them that love him." No matter what you may face in life, remember to put God first and to love him with all your mind, body, and soul, and in due season, you will receive your reward.

I'm still on my journey with the Lord and he is still refining me and increasing me in the things of him. There is no limit to God, he can do whatever he wants to do with his children. He can take a simple little man that people may look down on and do a great work in him. Take the limit off God and let him do the same for you. There was a time when I felt like I was being pushed aside and people didn't always see my true potential like I wanted them to. But the Lord saw me for who I really am and he saw something in me that no one else saw.

Before the eyes of God, we are seen as precious diamonds. The Father up in heaven loves his children and he cares for those who are mistreated and misunderstood. Trust in the Lord and never give up on your dreams and stay true to your calling and life's purpose regardless of life circumstances. Remember the Lord is always with you even until the end. Stay encouraged and keep your eyes fixed on the Lord. I hope my experiences, dreams, and testimonies has uplifted you and has given you a whole new perspective to life and its daily challenges. My name is Prophetess Rose Gordon and this is my life story as an "overcomer." God bless!

About the Author

Rose Gordon, born in Kingston, Jamaica, went through many struggles in her life. A single mother that raised three children on her own discovered that there is more to life when it's lived for God. Her testimony of how Jesus delivered her from depression, sicknesses, oppression, and loneliness, led her to share her story to others who are experiencing similar tests. Rose Gordon is a pastor, a prophetess, and a spiritual life coach. She wants both women and men from all over the world, single or married, with children or without children, to experience God for themselves because he is real. There's no limit to what the Lord can do in the lives of many who trust and believe in him. Rose Gordon is a living testimony. All the trials and temptations she has faced and overcome has molded her and shaped her into the woman that God wants her to be. Rose Gordon is an "overcomer," and she is also more than a conqueror. Up until this day, God continues to empower her to be all that he wants her to be in life.

Made in the USA
Middletown, DE
21 August 2023

36744768R00040